explaining

CEREBRAL PALSY

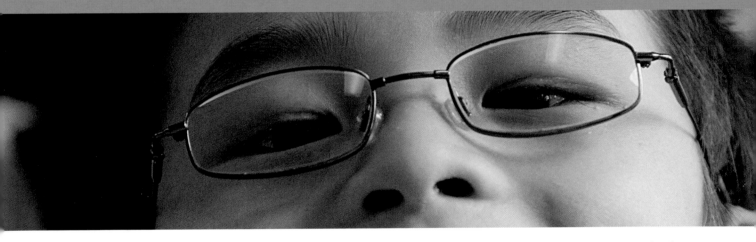

SARAH LEVETE

A+

Smart Apple Media

Smart Apple Media
P.O. Box 3263, Mankato, Minnesota 56002

Printed in the United States

Library of Congress Cataloging-in-Publication Data

Levete, Sarah.
  Explaining cerebral palsy / Sarah Levete.
    p. cm. – (Explaining–)
  Includes index.
  ISBN 978-1-59920-311-9 (hardcover)
  1. Cerebral palsy–Juvenile literature. I. Title.
  RC388.L48 2010
  616.8'36–dc22

                          2008049287

Published by arrangement with the Watts
Publishing Group Ltd, London.
Planning and production by Discovery Books
Limited
Managing Editor: Laura Durman
Editor: Annabel Savery
Designer: Keith Williams
Picture research: Rachel Tisdale
Consultant: Lindsay Brewis, Scope Early Years Team

Photo acknowledgements: Getty Images: p. 10 (Taxi);
istockphoto.com: p. 9 (digitalskillet); John Birdsall/
www.JohnBirdsall.co.uk: front cover all images, pp. 8, 11, 15,
17, 19, 20, 24, 25, 27, 28, 30, 31, 32, 34, 35, 36, 38; Phil
Jones/Medical College of Georgia: p. 39; Kristina Martinez: p.
37; Science Photo Library: p. 12 (CC Studio), p. 13 (Du Cane
Medical Imaging Ltd); Soundbeam/www.soundbeam.co.uk:
p. 23; Therasuit LLC: p. 18; University of Delaware: p. 22

Source credits: We would like to thank the following for
their contribution: University of Virginia Health Systems,
http://www.healthsystem.virginia.edu/internet/pediatrics/
patients/Tutorials/cp.cfm; Celine's new splints, by Celine and
Scope (p. 21); Japanese Technical Engineer with Cerebral
Palsy Works Effectively and Productively Using Her Computer,
Assistive Technology, and Built-in Windows Accessibility
Options, http://www.microsoft.com/enable/casestudy/oki.aspx,
17/04/08 (p. 25); http://www.ncl.ac.uk/sparcle/
publications_1.htm; Living with cerebral palsy, Susie Bennet,
http://www.livingwithcerebralpalsy.com; Disability Services
Queensland http://www.disability.qld.gov.au/community/
see-beyond/cerebral-palsy.html;
http://www.francescamartinez.com/html/flash_site.html;
http://www.cerebralpalsymagazine.com/

*Please note the case studies in this book are either true life
stories or based on true life stories.*

*The pictures in the book feature a mixture of adults
and children with and without cerebral palsy. Some of the
photographs feature models, and it should not be implied
that they have cerebral palsy.*

9 8 7 6 5 4 3 2 1

Contents

What is Cerebral Palsy?

You may well know someone with cerebral palsy, or perhaps you have cerebral palsy. Elderly people, adults, teenagers, young children, boys, girls—thousands of people have a condition called cerebral palsy. The term is often shortened to CP.

What Causes Cerebral Palsy?

The term cerebral palsy describes several different conditions caused by damage to a baby or young child's brain. The brain sends the wrong messages to muscles in the body. The muscles become too stiff or too floppy. This can result in difficulty moving, difficulty controlling movements, and difficulty stopping unwanted movements.

Different for Everyone

Aisha walks, runs and jumps, but she finds it hard to use her left arm to pick things up. Jacob is unable to walk or speak. Both of these children have cerebral palsy. Aisha's cerebral palsy is mild; Jacob's is severe. Cerebral palsy can affect the whole body, just one side, or one arm or leg. It affects everyone differently.

Some people with mild cerebral palsy live totally independent lives, perhaps only having difficulty holding a pen or kicking a football; others may not be able to walk at all. Cerebral palsy can also cause certain types of learning difficulties.

Cerebral palsy is not life-threatening, but it can have a devastating effect upon an individual and his or her family.

▼ *The effects of cerebral palsy are different for everyone.*

WORD ORIGINS

Cerebral comes from the Latin word *cerebrum* meaning brain; palsy comes from the Latin word *paralysis* which means the loss of the ability to move a body part.

▲ *Cerebral palsy can affect anyone regardless of sex or ethnic background.*

It is Not Catchable

A child is born with cerebral palsy, or develops it early in the first few years of life. Cerebral palsy is not a disease or illness; you cannot catch it from somebody else. It is not thought to be hereditary, although there is some research to show that there may be genetic links (see pages 38–39.)

The brain damage that causes cerebral palsy does not worsen, but some of the effects it has on the body can get worse. Many adults with cerebral palsy find that as they get older their muscles stiffen and may become harder to use. While cerebral palsy does not get worse, it does not go away either.

CEREBRAL PALSY CAN CAUSE

- Difficulty walking or moving
- Jerky, unwanted movements
- Slow physical development
- Speech difficulties
- Difficulty swallowing or chewing
- Balance problems
- Difficulty coordinating movements
- Difficulty learning

The Causes of Cerebral Palsy

Cerebral palsy results from damage to the brain. The damage can happen when babies are growing in the womb or in the first few years of life.

During the last few months of pregnancy, a fetus's brain grows very quickly. Hundreds of thousands of nerve cells are added to the fetus's brain every minute! These nerve cells are called neurons. They help the brain to do its job of controlling and coordinating the body and mind. Neurons send and receive messages from the brain and the rest of the body. By the time a baby is born, he or she has billions of neurons. Damaged neurons can cause cerebral palsy.

New Babies

Doctors cannot always pinpoint the exact cause of cerebral palsy because there are several reasons why a person may have the condition. Certain infections, such as rubella (German measles) and toxoplasmosis (caught from eating meat that is not cooked properly), can pass from a pregnant woman to her growing baby in the womb, damaging the fetus's brain.

Complications or problems during labor can also cause cerebral palsy. This happens if a baby's brain does not receive enough oxygen or if brain damage occurs during birth. Babies that are premature or very underweight are more at risk of developing cerebral palsy.

▼ *The brain develops rapidly in the womb and in the early years of life.*

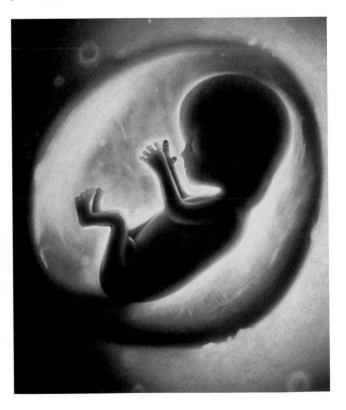

WHEN CEREBRAL PALSY OCCURS

Approximately 70 percent of cerebral palsy occurs during pregnancy, 20 percent during birth and 10 percent occurs during the first two years of life.

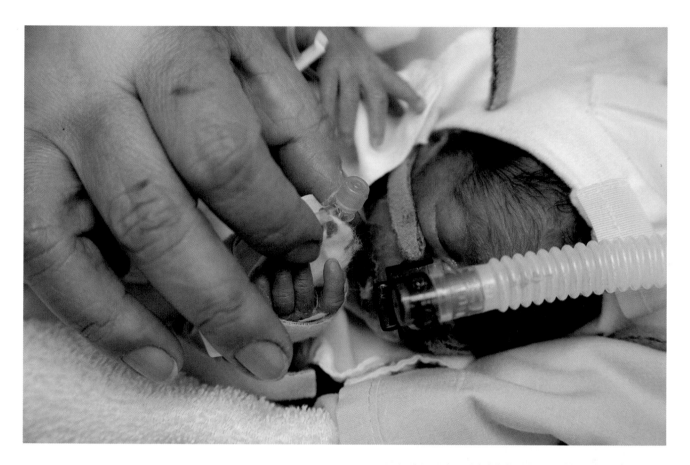

▲ *The organs of a premature baby are not fully developed and this increases the risk of injury to the brain and of developing cerebral palsy.*

Young Children

The brain develops an incredible amount in the first few years of life. By the time toddlers are about two years old their brains are roughly 80 percent of the size of an adult brain. Any damage to the brain during this time can cause cerebral palsy. For example, if a very young child catches an infection, such as meningitis, when the brain is still developing, there is a risk of cerebral palsy. The infection makes parts of the brain swell and this prevents enough oxygen reaching the brain.

CAN CEREBRAL PALSY BE PREVENTED?

There is no single cause of cerebral palsy so it is impossible to prevent. However, parents can reduce the risk of having a baby with cerebral palsy. Pregnant mothers should not smoke or take illegal drugs, and should avoid alcohol. All of these things are believed to damage the growth of neurons in an unborn baby. Improvements in maternity, prenatal and post-natal care all help to increase the chance of a safe and healthy birth for each baby.

Diagnosis

A newborn baby does little else apart from drink milk, cry, and sleep, but as the baby develops over the next few months, he or she begins to respond more by looking around, reaching for things, and trying to sit up.

Doctor's Diagnosis

If a baby is not showing these signs of development, a doctor may want to investigate further to see if there is a particular problem. With an early diagnosis, doctors can make sure that a child gets the best support early on. It is easier to control some problems caused by cerebral palsy if they are treated when the child is still young. For instance, exercises to help children stretch the muscles in their legs stop them from stiffening up permanently. However, cerebral palsy may not become obvious until a child is a few years old.

"I was 18 months old. The doctor stripped my clothing off, and he held me upside down, by my feet, watched the pattern of my body as I screamed, and everything went into spasm, and he said, 'This child is spastic. Take her home. Forget about her. She'll never be any good.'"

Dr. Lin Berwick MBE, counselor, lecturer, journalist, broadcaster, homeopath, Methodist preacher, Braille transcriber

The doctor's diagnosis of Dr. Lin Berwick was harsh and uncaring. Today's doctors use more sophisticated methods to diagnose cerebral palsy and are much aware of the needs of the baby and

family. Doctors and medical practitioners can now be given training to help them to break the news of a child's diagnosis to the family sensitively. The time of diagnosis can be very difficult for parents, and doctors provide a lot of support helping the parents to understand their child's condition and the care that they will need.

▼ *Doctors check the physical development of babies. Some early signs of cerebral palsy can be detected at these checkups.*

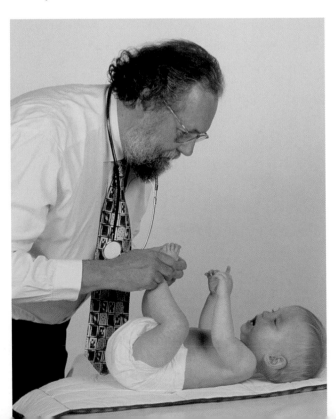

Observations

Doctors expect babies and children to be able to do certain things by a certain age. For instance, by six months, most babies can roll from back to tummy; by 18 months, most babies can pick up a cup and spoon. If a baby is unable to do this, or a young child is unable to stand or walk long after other children of their age are able to do so, the doctor might suspect that the child has cerebral palsy. The doctor can then arrange other tests.

Tests

Making a diagnosis is not always straightforward or immediate because the effects of cerebral palsy can take a while to become obvious, and because there are many symptoms associated with cerebral palsy. Doctors must be completely sure that they are making the right diagnosis, which means this process can take a long time. As well as observing a child's progress, there are certain tests that can be done to help doctors. These include CAT scans and MRI scans that take pictures of the brain's structure and can show any damaged areas. These pictures are taken using Magnetic Resonance Imaging (MRI) scanners. With a huge magnet, radio waves are sent to the body and back again. A computer changes the signals from the radio waves into pictures. Computed Axial Tomography (CAT scans) uses computers to create a 3-D image of what is going on inside the brain. It is very difficult for doctors to diagnose cerebral palsy in a child younger than six months without an MRI or CAT scan.

Although these scans can tell us where the brain is injured, they are not yet able to predict how the damage will affect a child in the future.

LITTLE'S DISEASE

In the 1860s, an English doctor named Dr. Little described a condition in which children had muscle problems, movement difficulties and twitching. The condition became known as "Little's disease." So-called Little's disease is today known as spastic cerebral palsy, one type of cerebral palsy (see pages 14–15).

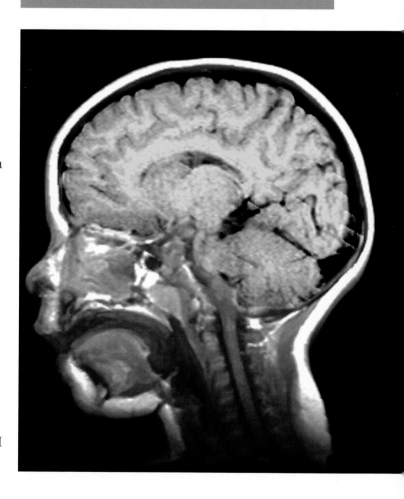

▲ *This is an MRI scan of a child's brain. A scan like this would show any damaged areas.*

Types of Cerebral Palsy

Stroke your cheek with your hand. Does your hand do what your brain has told it to do, or does your hand rise up suddenly and smack you on the cheek? A person with cerebral palsy may not be able to touch their cheek smoothly and with control because the brain does not coordinate the muscles properly, or the muscles are too floppy or stiff.

There are several types of cerebral palsy and a person may have one or more different types. The type of cerebral palsy depends upon which part of the brain is damaged.

Spastic Cerebral Palsy

This is the most common type of cerebral palsy. It mostly affects the muscles, making them stiff, weak, tight, or floppy. Muscles in the body help us make all kinds of movements, such as sitting up straight, turning the pages of a book, or holding a pen. When the muscles do not work properly, movement is limited. A child with spastic cerebral palsy may walk with one leg dragging, or on their toes. Sometimes, the legs make scissor-like movements.

Spasticity can affect one, two, three, or all four limbs, although two or four limbs are most commonly affected. When a person has all four limbs affected, the tightness in their muscles shows in their neck, face, and upper body, and it can also disrupt the working of their internal systems, such as their stomach, bladder, and bowel.

▶ *Damage to different parts of the brain causes different types of cerebral palsy.*

Athetoid Cerebral Palsy

A person with athetoid cerebral palsy is unable to control the movement of their muscles. This affects coordination. It can cause jerky movements or sudden floppiness. Athetoid cerebral palsy often also affects speech, hearing and digestion.

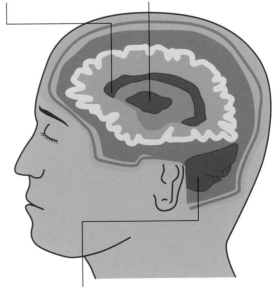

Cortex
Spastic cerebral palsy (spasticity). Disordered control of movement.

Basal Ganglia
Athetoid cerebral palsy (athetosis). Involuntary spasms, jerky arm and leg movements.

Cerebellum
Ataxic cerebral palsy (ataxia). Lack of balance and spacial awareness. Unsteady walking/gait.

▲ *This boy has athetoid cerebral palsy which makes his limbs move jerkily and with little control.*

Ataxic Cerebral Palsy

This type of cerebral palsy causes problems with balance and muscle coordination. People with ataxic cerebral palsy often walk with their legs wide apart and their hands and feet often shake. This shaking gets worse as their limbs move away from their body and so affects their ability to reach out for things in particular.

Whatever the symptoms or type of cerebral palsy a person has, it is important to think of the individual rather than the label "cerebral palsy."

Adult Brain Damage

If an adult has a bad accident and receives a blow to the head, he or she may suffer from brain damage. Brain damage that occurs when the brain has already fully developed is not the same as cerebral palsy. Some of the effects may be similar, but cerebral palsy refers to damage caused when the brain is still developing.

LANGUAGE

In the 1970s and 1980s, the word "spastic" became an insult and a term of abuse, used by people who did not understand physical disabilities or who did not consider or respect the feelings of people with any type of disability. The term spastic should only be used to describe a particular type of cerebral palsy.

Other Effects of Cerebral Palsy

Along with movement difficulties, cerebral palsy is often linked to other problems and medical conditions. Spasms, seizures, learning problems, visual problems, and speech problems are all effects of cerebral palsy. Cerebral palsy can also cause other problems in these areas.

Bones and Joints

The pull and push of the elastic-like muscles help bones develop. When muscles are too stiff or too weak, the bones that are linked to those muscles do not form properly. As a result, many people with cerebral palsy have bones that are out of position, twisted, or not fully developed and their joints may also be misshapen.

Sensing Space

The brain understands, or decodes, messages picked up by our senses. Brain damage often leaves the brain unable to decode these messages, so children with cerebral palsy often have visual difficulties. They may find it difficult to work out different shapes or to judge distances. A child may bump into things in the playground, or be unable to steer a wheelchair, even in a large space.

Communication

The brain translates ideas into words; sounds are formed in the larynx and palate, and then muscles in the cheek, tongue, and lips form words. When cerebral palsy affects these muscles, it makes it

DOES CEREBRAL PALSY AFFECT A PERSON'S INTELLIGENCE?

The answer to this question is sometimes and sometimes not. If a person is unable to walk or sit up straight, it does not necessarily mean that their ability to learn is any less than anyone else's. However, brain damage often affects areas of the brain that control learning ability. Consequently, some people with cerebral palsy may have learning difficulties. Some people are also unable to understand or reason fully—this is called intellectual impairment.

Just like any other group in the population, some people with cerebral palsy have no learning difficulties, some have mild learning difficulties, and some have severe learning difficulties.

hard to speak clearly. A person with cerebral palsy may slur words, speak very slowly, or speak with a jerky manner. Some people with cerebral palsy cannot speak at all. Others can speak, but may have difficulty with their memory or with finding the right words to use.

Hearing difficulties caused by cerebral palsy may also affect children's ability to communicate. It may be difficult for them to hear clearly, or they may be completely deaf.

Digestion

Children with cerebral palsy often have difficulties swallowing and digesting food because the muscles that control these actions may not receive the correct signals from the brain and therefore do not work correctly. Many children with cerebral palsy are underweight because of the physical difficulties experienced when eating and digesting food.

Epilepsy

When the brain sends muddled electrical messages around the body, it can create too much electrical activity. This can cause a person to have seizures. This condition is called epilepsy. More than one in three people with cerebral palsy will also have epilepsy.

The symptoms described on these pages can also affect people who do not have cerebral palsy.

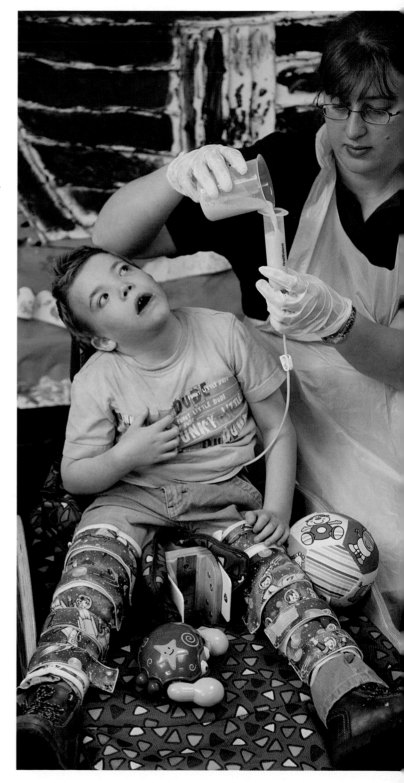

▶ *This boy is fed though a tube because his cerebral palsy prevents him from eating and digesting food normally.*

Managing Cerebral Palsy

There is no cure for cerebral palsy, but it can be managed so that the individual can live as independently as possible. Managing cerebral palsy can mean following a regular exercise program or learning how to use a wall for balance when getting up.

Physical Activity

Physical activity has huge benefits for everyone. Children with cerebral palsy are encouraged to do as much physical activity as possible. If they are helped to deal with the physical effects of their cerebral palsy, they will become more independent.

"If I don't do my exercises I seize up. I wouldn't be able to get myself out of bed and into my wheelchair."
Anna, age 19 with cerebral palsy

The Team

A team of specialists works on all the different aspects of a person's cerebral palsy, from walking difficulties to finding the right table to fit with a wheelchair. The team is made up of doctors, orthopedists, physiotherapists, occupational therapists, speech therapists, aides, and the family. The people in the team work together to help an individual manage life at home and school.

Physical Therapy

This is crucial for helping to manage cerebral palsy and to prevent deformities in bones and joints. A physical therapist uses physical exercises to help increase the strength and flexibility of muscles and limbs. These exercises also help posture and movement.

Some children wear body braces. The brace acts like an outer skeleton and gives extra support when children are exercising.

▼ *This girl, who has cerebral palsy, wears a special "suit" that puts specific pressure on certain parts of her body to help improve her movement and posture.*

▲ *It takes a lot of effort for this boy to walk a short distance, but the movement helps to stop his muscles and limbs from stiffening up.*

KELLY'S STORY

Kelly is an eighteen-year-old American with cerebral palsy. She has difficulty walking, speaking, and controlling her movements.

"Doctors said that I might never walk or talk and that I could be mentally retarded. They were wrong. I soon began having therapy many times each week to help me learn to speak and to move more easily. Although I walk differently and sometimes it is hard to understand what I'm saying, I can now do almost everything that other people can do. I have always been the only disabled student in my school and I have many friends. I like to listen to music, play on the computer, read books, and watch basketball. I can't wait to go to college because I will always be with my friends and my parents won't be there to tell me what to do. Also, I can study to be a teacher or counselor so that when I grow up I can help other disabled people and their families."

Some simple exercises, such as rolling over a large ball to help stretch and loosen up muscles, can be done every day at home. Other exercises, such as exercising while hanging in the air using bungee jumping-type equipment, need expert assistance and a special apparatus.

Occupational Therapy

Occupational therapists give advice on how to manage daily life at home, school or work. They provide equipment such as a chair with head support so that someone with a floppy neck can look straight ahead, or an angled keyboard so a person can use a computer. If the physical effects of cerebral palsy make it hard to tie shoe laces or lift a cup, an occupational therapist can help the individual find a way to perform such everyday activities.

Other Support

There are many different treatments for cerebral palsy. None can cure the condition, but each has its own role and benefits for the individual.

Drugs

Some drugs help to release muscle tension or tightness. These include botox, which is more widely used in the form of injections to get rid of wrinkles. People with cerebral palsy are given botox to losen stiff muscles.

▼ *Working with his physical therapist and wearing special leg braces, this boy practices exercises to develop his muscles and movement.*

Sometimes a pump is fitted into a person's body in an operation. The pump releases drugs directly towards the spinal cord to relax the muscles. This gives the person immediate relief from pain caused by muscle spasms. Even though these drugs can help relieve the pain of muscle tension for a while, it is important to continue with long-term treatments, such as physical therapy.

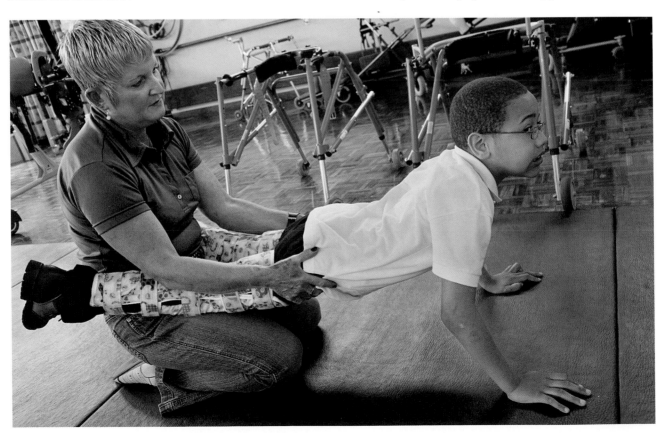

In the 1930s, Hungarian doctor Andras Peto developed a technique to help people with motor (movement) difficulties called "conductive education." This intensive program combines physical, emotional and learning skills. It is based on Peto's belief that the repetition of movements and tasks helps the brain send messages to the muscles to create movement.

Gait Analysis

Sometimes, people with cerebral palsy are filmed as they walk along a set path. Computers analyze the information and the results provide detailed information about the muscles they use and the precise way in which they walk. This is called gait analysis. Specialists look at the information and use it to decide which type of treatment is most appropriate for the individual, from an operation to physical therapy.

Working on Bones

An orthopedist is a bone specialist who decides if a person needs treatment to help correct the position of bones or muscles. Wearing splints or braces against particular bones can help straighten and support legs and arms.

For a few individuals with cerebral palsy, an operation is necessary to correct or improve their comfort and mobility. Twisted bones in the legs,

CASE NOTES

CELINE'S STORY

Celine is eight years old and wears leg splints to help her walk and stand. She says: "They are made of plastic and keep your feet and ankles in a good position. Lots of children wear them too, even my friend Oran. His splints are different from mine and don't have any hinges. You wear the splints over your socks and then put your shoes on top. I didn't want to wear them at first....I tried them on and it felt funny at first and then I had to practice wearing them for a bit every day. I had to say if it rubbed. After about a week I started to wear them all day. Oran wears his for a few hours at a time. ... Of course we wear them when we are sitting down but also when we are riding our bikes, and we wear them to the park, when we go shopping, to parties, and to school. Everywhere!"

hips, feet, or knees can be repositioned during an operation and metal plates are used to keep the bones in their new position. There are also operations to straighten a curved spine, which often affects people with cerebral palsy. This type of surgery is only performed on children because their bones are not yet fully developed and it is easier to move them into different positions.

Technological Support

From mini robots to specially adapted pens, there is an incredible range of devices, aids, and equipment that can transform the lives of people with cerebral palsy.

Available Technology

The development of computer-aided technology has meant huge advances in the support available to people with cerebral palsy. However, this equipment is not cheap—which means that it is not always available to people who need it.

In poorer parts of the world where there may be little access to specialist support, a person with cerebral palsy may be unable to reach their full potential. However, in other parts of the world, a person with similar disabilities caused by cerebral palsy may be able to move around and work easily with the assistance of technical equipment.

"In a nation of technological riches, there is no better way for engineers to use their creative talents than to find new methods and devices that help children with cerebral palsy overcome their daily barriers."

Richard Foulds, PhD, associate professor in the Biomedical Engineering Department at NJIT (New Jersey Institute of Technology).

Mini Robots

Young, non-disabled children learn to explore the world through discovery, by crawling, then walking around. Young children with cerebral palsy who have little or no movement cannot explore their world in this way—until now. Mini robots allow them the freedom to move around freely and safely. A child sits on the small robot and uses controls to guide the robot around. The robot is also fitted

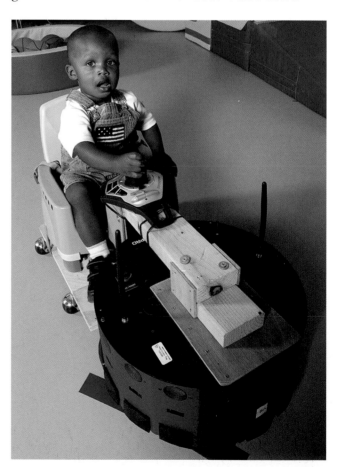

▲ *This boy can explore the world around him using a mini robot.*

with sensors that "sense" any obstacles that are in the way. The robot allows the child to bump into things safely or it can steer the child around them.

Until now, most children have only been provided with wheelchairs when they are about five years old. This is because wheelchairs can be difficult to handle. The mini robot acts like a parent or caregiver's guiding hand and can be used easily by a child under the age of five.

Electronic Wheelchairs

Many wheelchairs for older children and adults are fitted with electronic devices to make them easy to operate. At the push of a button, the wheelchair can turn to a particular position. Some switches can be turned on and off by the user by sipping or puffing air into a straw if movement is limited.

Sound Beams

Twenty years ago, if a young person could not hold an object, they would not have been able to play a musical instrument. Today it is possible to turn movement into sound using Soundbeam technology.

A tiny movement, such as the shake of a head or a wiggle of a finger, interrupts an invisible sound beam that is sent across a room or space. The sound beam sends a message to an instrument, such as an electronic keyboard, and it turns the message into a note or cord.

▼ *This boy is using Soundbeam technology to express himself through music and sound. This device uses ultrasonic sensors to detect movement, such as the nod of a head, and translates it, through a keyboard, into electronic music.*

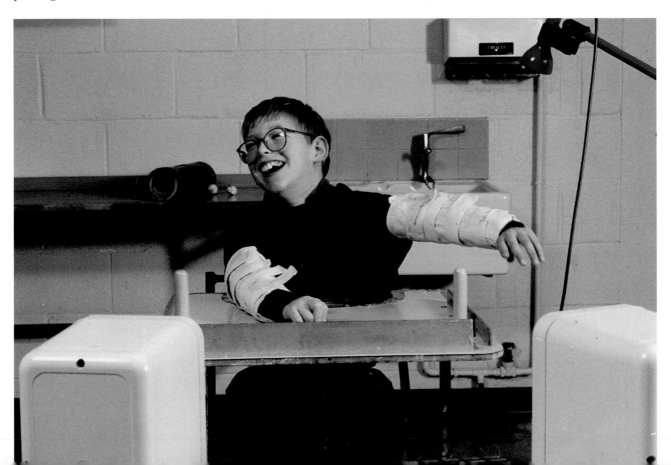

Communication

Many children with cerebral palsy have difficulty communicating. Their speech can be slurred or they may be unable to hear. They may also be unable to use body language to communicate.

Difficulty Communicating

It can be very difficult for a child to show evidence of understanding if they are unable to speak or communicate.

Twitches, unusual facial movements, or slurred speech are often characteristic of a person with cerebral palsy. They are not signs of learning difficulties, but people sometimes wrongly assume that this is the case.

▼ *This child is using pictures to communicate with his aide.*

There are many people with cerebral palsy who are extremely intelligent. Some may not be able to communicate verbally, but they find other ways to communicate, such as using sign language or computer technology. Young children who have difficulty chewing and swallowing often have difficulty developing speech. They can communicate using picture symbols that represent words and actions. Pointing to the relevant picture communicates the thoughts of that child.

Speaking Computers

Today, advances in technology help even the youngest children to communicate their thoughts and feelings. People with little or no ability to speak can use a machine made of a computer and voice synthesizer to turn movement into speech. A special light is attached to a headband. Head movements control the computer and the computer translates the movements from the light into speech.

If a person has slurred speech that is difficult to understand, special software programs can interpret the person's speech patterns. The computer repeats clearly what the user has said.

Speech Therapy

Speech therapy is important in helping a child to develop their speech or to learn another form of communication. A speech therapist uses exercises to help strengthen the muscles in the throat and jaw. If a child has no speech (or hearing) a speech therapist can teach them

different forms of communication, such as sign language or lip-reading.

▼ *A speech therapist helps this boy develop his spoken communication skills.*

How It Feels

Everyone experiences down days, off days, good days, and moody days. This could be due to friendship problems, trouble with a teacher, or an argument with a brother or sister. For people with cerebral palsy, there are additional factors that can affect mood and behavior.

Exhaustion

For someone without cerebral palsy, running a long distance is exhausting—it is tiring and takes a lot of effort. For some people with cerebral palsy it takes a lot of effort and energy just to get from one side of a room to the other. Small movements, such as holding a pen, can be exhausting, both physically and emotionally. It takes a lot of effort.

Challenges

The challenges presented by physical disabilities can make it difficult for a person to see value in him or herself. If others are unkind towards people because of their disability, it can be upsetting and isolating. It is unacceptable for anyone to behave in this way. People should support each other, whatever their strengths and weaknesses are. Unkind behavior can be particularly upsetting for

HAPPY CHILDREN

A research study in 2007 shows that the majority of children with cerebral palsy feel as happy as any other children. The study carried out by the University of Newcastle, England, asked 500 children with cerebral palsy for their views about the quality of their life. Most of the children said that they felt as happy as children without physical disabilities. Researchers found that children with cerebral palsy see their condition as part of themselves and embrace life with as much excitement as other children.

"Pity and sorrow should not be directed to disabled children, because our findings indicate that they experience most of life as do non-disabled children. Therefore, maximum effort is needed to support social and educational policies that recognize the similarity between the lives of disabled children and those of other children and that ensure their rights as citizens, rather than as disabled children, to participate fully in society."

Heather O. Dickinson, PhD.

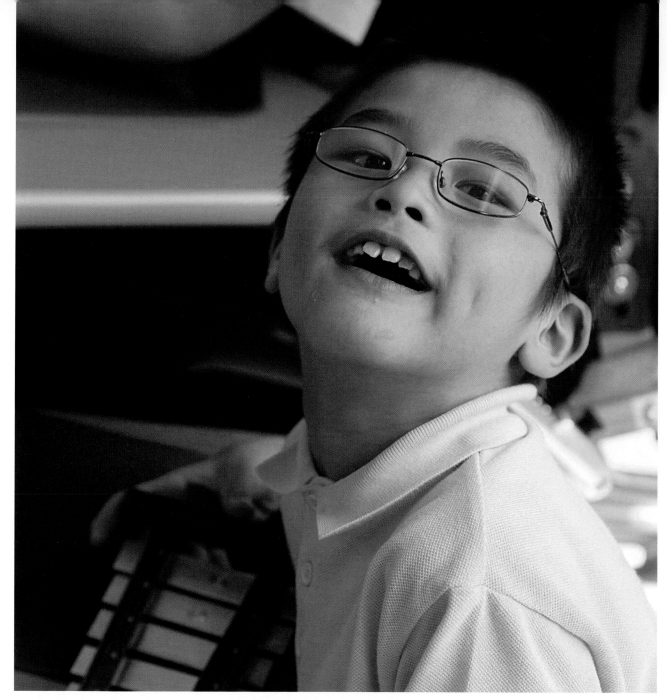

▲ *Physical disabilities present challenges and difficulties, but are not necessarily a barrier to a child's happiness.*

people with cerebral palsy. They are more likely to feel anxiety and stress in these situations because of the way their brain has been affected.

Dealing with Prejudice

"I have to work twice as hard at everything to prove myself."
Claire, student with cerebral palsy

Today, people with disabilities have rights that are recognized by the law. Even so, this does not stop some people from unfairly judging those who are disabled, or from treating them badly. An employer may only offer basic work to a person with cerebral palsy, even though the person is as capable as anyone else. Such prejudices and low expectations can be demoralizing and distressing.

Everyday Life

Everyday actions such as getting out of bed, using the restroom, and getting on the bus to school can feel like enormous hurdles to a person with cerebral palsy, and that is before the school day even begins! For some people who have severe cerebral palsy, these everyday activities can only be done with the support of a caregiver.

▼ *Cerebral palsy affects everyone in different ways. This girl is able to live and study independently. Others with severe physical disabilities and learning difficulties will need the support of an assistant throughout their lives.*

ALISON'S DAY

Alison has cerebral palsy. It affects her legs and her right arm. She lives with her mom and older brother.

"I really struggle waking up. Sometimes it's hard to sleep because my legs hurt so I'm tired in the morning. I get myself out of bed and into my wheelchair. My room is on the ground floor. We had to take out most of the doorways so I can get around the house.

Mom drives me to school. I go there with my brother. He races off to meet his friends but I'm still getting out of the car with the wheelchair. I've got a couple of really good mates [friends] at school. Some kids just don't bother with me—it's like being in a wheelchair makes me invisible or else they think I've got the plague!

There are a few other kids at school with different disabilities so it's quite well set up. I've got a special board to help me keep my paper in place. My handwriting is really rubbish [terrible] because I can't hold a pen properly, and sometimes I use a laptop when my hand gets tired. Sometimes I get headaches because I've got to concentrate so much and my eyes get tired. But the teachers are quite good. They give me small chunks of work at a time. I get extra time to do tests too.

Break time is great. Getting outside in the fresh air. I've got quite good at whizzing round in my chair. I've got this really cool motorized chair now but the other one was really hard work on my arms.

When I want to go to a friend's house, I have to get a lift, but I can't go in anyone's car—it's got to be a car that can fit a wheelchair inside. Everything just takes more effort for everyone. Sometimes I feel left out.

Every other week I have a session with the physiotherapist. She's great but she makes me work really hard, doing different exercises—loads of stretches.

When I get home, I have to do homework and my exercises. I've got some weights I use to strengthen my arms. That gets really boring but I know if I don't do it, it will get harder to move. Everything seems to take me much longer than the others. It really makes me cross when I go out with friends and we can't get my chair on the pavement.

Sometimes me and my brother argue. He gets fed up with all the attention I get— but I'd much prefer to be in his position. On the whole though, he's really ok and sticks up for me if anyone is giving me any grief at school."

Being at School

Reading from the board, using a pen, getting to a class: these are the basic things that you may take for granted at school. They can present great challenges to a person with cerebral palsy.

Different Schools

Some children with cerebral palsy go to a public, mainstream school; others go to a specialty school. There are advantages and disadvantages with each type of school, depending on the individual and his or her needs.

▼ *This boy is celebrating his exam success at school.*

If the effects of cerebral palsy are severe, and the person cannot communicate, eat independently, or move without help, he or she will need intensive support and care. If the effects are less severe and children can manage daily tasks without assistance, they should be able to attend a public school where they will get extra support when needed.

"Education is a basic human right."
UNICEF

Choosing a School

In a public school, children of all abilities mix and learn together. Disabled and non-disabled children can benefit greatly from being at school together. They can support each other and learn from each other. The mix of children encourages them to accept and understand that everyone is different and has different needs. This helps reduce the prejudice around disabilities. Many schools have departments that provide support for disabled pupils and parents can check what provisions are in place and whether they meet their child's needs.

▼ *This boy is using a computer to translate his eye and head movements into letters on a screen that his teacher can read.*

GLEN'S STORY

Glen has used a wheelchair all his life. He is now 21 and is about to live on his own and start work for a disability advice organization. Glen has cerebral palsy that affects his eyesight and the movement on the left-hand side of his body. Glen can get himself from a chair or bed to a wheelchair without help. At one mainstream school, Glen was told that lessons were on the second floor. He was given ten minutes to get to the classroom before the stampede of other kids. By the time he had struggled upstairs, he was exhausted and in no mood to concentrate. He then had to leave the lesson ten minutes early to get back downstairs.

In a specialty school, the facilities and teaching will be tailored to the needs of the children. All the rooms are adapted for wheelchair access. Tables are all set at suitable heights. The toilets are fitted with hoists to help children get on and off the toilet. Computers are set up with speech programs. Switches and handles are installed at a level to be within reach of a wheelchair user. Playgrounds are fitted with equipment for children of all physical abilities to enjoy and use.

Socializing

It is not easy to hang around and chat if your legs ache with the effort of standing in one position, or to get from one place to another to meet up with friends at break time if it takes effort and time to walk. It is important that others understand the needs of a person with a disability, such as cerebral palsy, and do not exclude them from social events simply because of physical challenges.

Cerebral Palsy and the Family

A diagnosis of cerebral palsy can have a major impact on a family. Any impairment or condition that affects a person's physical or learning ability affects everyone in the family—not just the person with the impairment.

Parents' Role

When parents are told that their child has cerebral palsy, it may be a great shock. They may blame themselves for their child's condition. They may worry that they will be unable to cope with looking after a disabled child.

Parents and caregivers have a huge role to play in the development of a child with cerebral palsy. Early support and education in managing day-to-day tasks, such as sitting up or holding a cup, can make a great difference to a child's progress. The responsibility for this is usually with the main caregivers, often a parent or parents. Looking after a child with special needs can be challenging, and caregivers of children with severe cerebral palsy will need emotional and practical support. It can be tiring and lonely for single parents, and they will need a lot of support from family and friends.

What about Me?

Brothers and sisters often feel jealous of each other. They may think that a brother or sister gets more attention than they do, but this is common in every family.

▼ *The physical and emotional support of family and friends can make a huge difference to a person caring for someone with cerebral palsy.*

In a family where one child depends upon, and needs, extra support and attention from parents, a brother or sister without cerebral palsy may feel left out. On the other hand, a child limited by his or her physical ability, or with special needs, may feel jealous of a brother or sister who is able to run around freely. It is important for young people in this situation to talk to parents or caregivers about their feelings.

Brothers and sisters can be incredibly supportive and helpful towards a family member with cerebral palsy. They can encourage and guide their sibling, but as in all families, there may also be tensions.

"…Many of the needs of the child with cerebral palsy are the same as those of the normal child. They need the love and affection of their families, and the opportunity that a home gives to explore their full potential."

Martin Bax, consultant pediatrician, Chelsea and Westminster Hospital

At Home

Houses need to be adapted so that a disabled child can move about as safely and as easily as possible. The type of equipment a house may need will depend on the needs of the individual. For example, wheelchairs are wide so doors in homes may need to be made wider. Wheelchair ramps or rails for a child to hold onto may be needed. These adaptations can be costly and parents may have difficulty accessing enough money to pay for them. Some organizations or local programs can provide financial assistance for families who need to adapt their homes.

JULIA'S STORY

Julia is a single parent and is the primary carergiver for her eight-year-old daughter, Hannah, who has cerebral palsy.

"[Every morning] I carry Hannah downstairs to breakfast. It's getting harder to carry her now that she's older… I make her porridge for breakfast and have to spoon-feed her myself. It takes about an hour because it has to be slow and steady. Hannah can't move—she can't feed herself, talk or walk. I generally give her two choices of outfits [every morning] and she uses noises to tell me which one she wants to wear. Sounds and eye movement are her only ways of communicating."

Hannah attends school at the Hornsey Trust and Conductive Education Center. "It's brilliant and follows the same curriculum as mainstream schools but it's coupled with speech and language work, occupational therapy and physiotherapy. Hannah is very competitive and motivated. She longs to be independent and can get frustrated with life—especially when she can't follow her little buddies when they all run off to play."

"No parent wants to see their child in pain or unhappy… I never think "Why me?" but I often think "Why Hannah?". It seems so horribly unfair. Yes, she's hard work. Very hard work. But she's an incredible little girl and I'm so proud of her. I feel lucky to have Hannah as my beautiful daughter."

Into Adulthood

Every day you will see men and women of all ages and abilities. Some of those adults, perhaps working in the bank or at the grocery store, may have cerebral palsy. Many adults with cerebral palsy live full and independent lives. Others need care and support their entire lives.

Fifty years ago, the future for children with cerebral palsy was bleak. Today, the outlook is much more positive, thanks to medical advances and improvements in understanding and treatments. Many people with cerebral palsy will continue to live well into their old age.

At Home and Work

Living independently is hard if you cannot reach a switch or turn a handle. There are many ways to adapt a home so that a person with movement difficulties can live on their own. A remote control can operate switches to turn on lights, heaters, and, of course, the television. Laser beam switches are turned on or off when the light beam is broken by the movement of a hand or shake of the head.

People with disabilities have the right to work and employers should provide a working space which meets the needs of any disabled employee. However, this is not always the case and it can be difficult to enforce.

More awareness of disability issues has led to increased access for disabled people. For instance, in many parts of the world, buses must be able to carry wheelchairs. However, people with mobility problems continue to have difficulties on public transport.

Support

Parents generally look after a child with cerebral palsy, but as those parents get older, they will be unable to look after their child in the same way. Helping a small child to move around or wash is much easier than helping an adult.

◀ *Cerebral palsy does not necessarily affect a person's ability to work.*

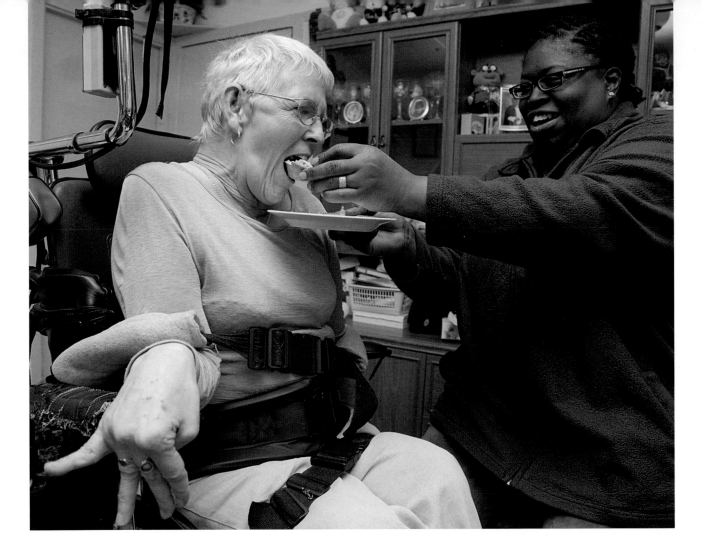

Depending on the degree of the disability, some people with cerebral palsy will need care and support in adult life. This may be in an accommodation where there are helpers who encourage independent living. If the person has severe cerebral palsy and needs constant care, they may need assistance eating, using the restroom, washing, and moving around.

Families

"I didn't know people like you could have babies!" Shop assistant to a pregnant woman with cerebral palsy. Laurence Clark, Ouch web site

Many adults with cerebral palsy go on to have their own families. Depending on the nature of their cerebral palsy, some may need extra support, but others are able to care for their children just as any other parents.

▲ *A person with severe cerebral palsy will need support and care to carry out everyday activities such as eating.*

Simple adjustments to equipment can make a huge difference when coping with a young baby and a disability. For instance, a stroller can attach to a mobility scooter, or cribs and changing tables can be built at a certain height for a wheelchair user to reach.

Getting Older

Cerebral palsy does not worsen with age, however the effects of aging may show sooner in adults with cerebral palsy. They can often develop medical conditions, such as arthritis, earlier than other adults might. Their physical ability may decrease and they may find that joints stiffen and flexibility is reduced. This can be helped with regular exercise and stretches.

Raising Awareness

Fifty years ago, disabled people had few rights and little status in society. Today, in most developed countries, the law recognizes the rights of any person with any type of disability.

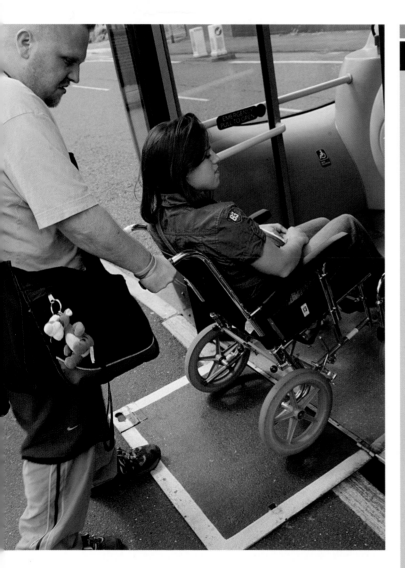

▲ *People have campaigned to make public transport accessible for wheelchair users.*

A DIFFICULT CASE

Ann Thorpe's daughter, Katie, has severe cerebral palsy. She cannot move independently, cannot feed herself, and has no control over her bladder or bowel. Fifteen-year old Katie also has severe intellectual impairment. Her mother wanted her daughter to have a hysterectomy. This is an operation to remove Katie's womb. A hysterectomy would prevent Katie from having monthly periods and from having children. Ann Thorpe wanted to protect her daughter from what she saw as the upset of experiencing periods which would cause Katie confusion and physical discomfort. Many people opposed Ann Thorpe's case and argued that there should be laws to protect disabled people from this sort of unnecessary operation. The local hospital authority decided to refuse the operation.

In such cases it is very difficult to make decisions about what is best for a person who is unable to communicate for themselves.

MARY'S STORY

Mary is a part-time administrative assistant and plans to study for a degree in social work. She believes that one way to manage cerebral palsy is to give some advice to people who do not have it, such as:

- Make an effort to communicate with people with cerebral palsy. Don't feel bad if you don't understand what they say—it's ok to ask them to repeat themselves.

- Allow an individual with cerebral palsy more time to undertake tasks, to communicate, and to move about.

- Remember that the effects of cerebral palsy differ greatly from one individual to another. Do not make assumptions about what people can and can't do.

▲ *Francesca Martinez is a comedian and actress.*

"I just see myself as a different set of cans and can'ts. I can't run, I can't drink through a straw, but I can stand on stage and tell jokes—I can do things other people can't do."
Francesca Martinez, actress with cerebral palsy.

Disablism

Disablism is when people treat unfairly anyone with a disability—because of the disability. It may range from name-calling or teasing to denying a person the opportunity to study at college. Today, there is an active disability rights movement. Many people campaign for better rights for disabled people—from access to transport to the right to go to work—and more support for carers of severely disabled children and adults.

Get Involved

You too can work to protect the rights of disabled people. Perhaps you have a disability, such as cerebral palsy, or know someone who has special needs. Stand up for the rights of everyone to be treated fairly and respectfully.

The Future

So far there is no cure for cerebral palsy, nor is there any way of preventing it. However, medical and technical advances have already transformed the lives of people with cerebral palsy. From scientists to engineers, experts are researching ways to prevent cerebral palsy and to further improve the lives of those with cerebral palsy.

Genes

Doctors now believe that there may be a link between genes and cerebral palsy. Genes are the building blocks of an individual's physical makeup and control the way each organ in the body functions. If there is a faulty gene, perhaps inherited from a parent, it could be a cause of cerebral palsy. Scientists are trying to identify these genes that may be responsible for causing cerebral palsy.

What About a Vaccine?

Scientists, doctors, and researchers are working to understand more precisely the causes of cerebral palsy. There is some research looking into the connection between the herpes virus, which causes common cold sores, and the onset of cerebral palsy. If doctors are able to identify the exact cause, then they can target ways to prevent it, perhaps with a vaccine.

FACTS AND FIGURES

- In the U.S. more than 750,000 people have cerebral palsy.

- 1 in every 500 babies has cerebral palsy in the United Kingdom.

- There are more than 17,000,000 people with cerebral palsy worldwide.

▶ *Medical and technical advances have transformed the lives of people with cerebral palsy.*

STEM CELLS

So far, doctors have not discovered a way to repair the brain once damage has occurred.

Scientists are researching ways to grow new cells in the brain to replace the damaged ones. In China, doctors are using stem cells from healthy babies which they insert into the spinal cord of babies with cerebral palsy. The stem cells are thought to grow into new cells to replace the damaged ones in the brain.

Stem cell research is a hotly debated issue as the research often involves using cells from human embryos.

▲ *Doctors like Dr. Borlongan are in the early stages of investigating the benefits of stem cell therapy for children with cerebral palsy.*

Electronic Boots

Engineers are working with bone specialists to design boots that can record information about how a person walks and moves. Physical therapists will be able to analyze the information to design further exercises to improve a person's movement.

In future developments, modern electronics and nanotechnology will be used to create equipment that will further transform the abilities of those with cerebral palsy.

Awareness in Society

Life for those with cerebral palsy in the 21st century is very different from just 50 years ago. There is much more understanding and awareness of the condition. People with cerebral palsy are more accepted.

Cara Readle is a young actress. She happens to have cerebral palsy. One of Cara's recent roles is playing a girl called Layla in a popular TV show. Layla has cerebral palsy. It is not the main feature of her character, though.

Perhaps in years to come, having an actor on television who happens to have cerebral palsy will not be so unusual.

Glossary

arthritis a condition that affects the joints in the body

ataxic cerebral palsy a type of cerebral palsy caused by damage to the cerebellum, which causes problems with balance and muscle coordination

athetoid cerebral palsy a type of cerebral palsy caused by damage to the basal ganglia, which causes a person to have difficulties controlling muscle movements

basal ganglia a part of the brain that controls coordination of movement

bio-medical engineering using engineering principles to solve medical problems

braces a device fitted to an arm or leg to give support

CAT scans Computed Axial Tomography which uses computers to take three-dimensional images of the inside of the brain

cerebellum part of the brain at the back of the skull that coordinates muscle activity

cerebral palsy a term used to describe a range of difficulties, mainly affecting movement, that are caused by brain damage

cerebrum part of the brain, located in the front area of the skull

conductive education a specialized program of exercises designed to help people with movement disabilities such as cerebral palsy

cortex part of the brain that forms the outer layer of the cerebrum

deteriorate worsen

developed countries a country that is advanced economically and socially

diagnosis identification of a particular condition, such as cerebral palsy

embryo a fetus in its earliest stage of development

epilepsy a condition in which a person has fits or seizures caused by overactivity in the brain

fetus a baby that is in its last stages of development in the mother's womb

gait the way a person stands and walks

genes the basic unit of heredity by which characteristics are passed from one generation to the next

genetic influenced by genes inherited from parents

hereditary passed from parent to child

impairment a weakness or damage

labor when a baby is being born

larynx a hollow organ at the top of your windpipe that holds your vocal chords

maternity motherhood

meningitis swelling in a part of the brain caused by an infection that can cause headaches, fever, sensitivity to light, stiff muscles and, in severe cases, death

motor difficulties difficulties with movement

MRI scans Magnetic Resonance Imaging which takes computerized images of the inside of the body using radio waves

nanotechnology technology that is designed with the most miniature materials

neuron a brain cell

occupational therapy practical advice and exercises to support a person in daily life

orthopedist a bone specialist

pediatrician a doctor who specializes in treating children

palate the roof of the mouth

physiotherapist someone who teaches special exercises to people with movement difficulties in order to improve muscle function

physiotherapy special exercises to improve muscle function

postnatal after birth

prejudice judging someone unfairly

premature a baby born before the 35th week of pregnancy

prenatal before birth

rubella a disease that is a mild form of measles, and is also known as German measles

spastic cerebral palsy a type of cerebral palsy that is caused by damage to the cortex, which causes muscles to be stiff, weak, tight or floppy

speech therapist someone who helps people with speech and language difficulties

speech therapy a program for people who have difficulties with communication and language

spinal cord the bundle of nerves inside the spine, or backbone, that connects nearly all parts of the body to the brain

splint a strip of stiff material used to support a bone and to hold it in a fixed position

stem cell a cell from which other cells can develop

toxoplasmosis a disease that may be caused by eating undercooked meat, symptoms may not show in adults but are dangerous to unborn babies

voice synthesizer a computer that changes movements or signals into speech

womb an organ in the lower body of a woman where babies grow and develop

Further Information

Books

Cerebral Palsy

by Ruth Bjorklund, Marshall Cavendish
Benchmark, 2007

Children with Cerebral Palsy : a Manual for Therapists, Parents and Community Workers

by Archie Hinchcliffe, *Thousand Oaks: SAGE Publications*, 2007.

Physical Therapy of Cerebral Palsy

by Freeman Miller, *Springer*, 2007

Trends in cerebral palsy research

Edited by Helen D. Fong, *Nova Science Publishers*, 2006

Organizations

Canadian Cerebral Palsy Sports Association

www.ccpsa.ca
1-866-247-9934

Children's Hemiplegia and Stroke Assn. (CHASA)

www.hemi-kids.org
(817) 492-4325

Children's Neurobiological Solutions (CNS) Foundation

www.cnsfoundation.org
1-866-CNS-5580 (267-5580) 805-898-4442

Easter Seals

www.easterseals.com
1-800-221-6827

March of Dimes Foundation

www.marchofdimes.com
1- 888-MODIMES (663-4637)

Pathways Awareness Foundation [For Children With Movement Difficulties]
www.pathwaysawareness.org
1-800-955-CHILD (2445)

Pedal with Pete [For Research on Cerebral Palsy]
www.pedalwithpete.com
1-800-304-PETE (7383)

United Cerebral Palsy (UCP)
www.ucp.org
1-800-USA-5UCP (872-5827)

United Cerebral Palsy (UCP) Research & Educational Foundation
www.ucpresearch.org
1-800-USA-5UCP (872-5827)

Web Sites

www.kidshealth.org/kid/health_problems/
brain/cerebral_palsy.html
Information for children about cerebral palsy from the Kids Health web site.

www.ninds.nih.gov/disorders/cerebral_palsy/
cerebral_palsy.htm
Information about cerebral palsy from the National Institute of Neurological Disorders and Stroke.

Note to Parents and Teachers: Every effort has been made by the publishers to ensure that these web sites are suitable for children, that they are of the highest educational value, and that they contain no inappropriate or offensive material. However, because of the nature of the Internet, it is impossible to guarantee that the contents of these sites will not be altered. We strongly advise that Internet access is supervised by a responsible adult.

Index

Titles and Contents in Explaining . . .